For The Buckley
Family

For teaching
Me to never
stop fighting

For the Love of
My God, Mama

母

以心伝以

Poems by Matt Cooper

Spartan Press

Kansas City   Missouri

Spartan Press

Kansas City, Missouri

spartanpresskc.com

Acknowledgments:

Mom, thank you for teaching me that despite the sadistic nature of life, all things are feasible. In the end, you will always be the hero I needed. Though we may wind up frayed and in pieces from time to time, the brokenness provoking us to flee to the outskirts of our world in order to heal and breathe for a time, knowing that though where we come from there are no oceans or mountains—the land being wiser than us—we revolve back to the moment of impact, knowing that through our secret way of love and understanding, it is you and me against the world.

Gran Pat and Grandpa Lonnie, you are both my grandparents. For better or worse, it is your blood that runs through me and it is my filial duty to be grateful for that. I love you both.

Don Adlesperger, you have invested in me many times over and these days that inspiration has me in the habit of investing in myself.

Shaune Larder, you are the only solipsist I have ever respected. Thanks for helping me find my super power.

Also, I would like to thank Kaeley Hansen, Alex, Brent, Jessica, Larry, Julie, and Neil Buckley, Michael Cissell, Dylan Ramos, Breck and Emily Adkins, Addison McLaughlin, Clayton Walter, Bobby Holbrook, Amy Chastain, Michael Swan, Freda Briggs, Albert Goldbarth, Heather Fangmann, Rob Klem, Jeff Tymony, Steve Chen, Austin and Ann Alexander, Brian Hayes, Julie Clements, Ichiro and Hibiki Kato, Jennifer Musaji, Abu Diabo, Kandwani Mwale, Ashim from Nepal, Iitsuka Miho, Suzuna Abo, Yumi Foster, Nishimura Yoshihisa, Yoshikawa Junzo, Matsuri Sakai, Chance Swaim, Amy DeVault, John Darr, Matt Kelly, Kylie Cameron, Evan Pflugradt, Christian Yost, Hannah England, Michelle Lord, Anthony Patterson, Matt Noyes, Chauncey Stangle, Oliva Vest, Dom Brown, Chris Wheatley, Brett Petty, Nick Fowler, Genero

Garcia, Andi Stipp, Aaron Evans, Art Torez, Chad Gaudet, Rebecca Bechtold, Matt Clagg, Nanako and Namiki, Ann Burger, Braxton Koehler, Grandma Bodine, Rebecca Petchenik, Harold Bise, Debbie Dastidar, Mr. Green from Astronomy 101, Eli Graves, Brady Farner, Jimmy Montgomery, Carmen, Vincent and Tano Triana, Teresa Mayginnes, Karen Kinder, John and Brandi Anderson, Jim and Jane Cooper, James Montgomery, Nip, Tuck and Skip Morgan, Hia Trahn, Cassy Deleon, Richard Jones, The Butler Lantern, and the City of Katano, Osaka, Japan.

Finally, I want to thank my brother Tim. You are twice the writer and twice the man that I will ever be.

"For the Dogs", "De Rerum Natura with a Handgun", "Caucasian and Homeless in Beijing", and "Logic of Wind", previously appeared in the *Butler Lantern*.

"Lost and Found at the Fall Matsuri", appeared in the spring 2019 issue of *Mikrokosmos*.

This, my first book, was written while living in the beautiful traditional Heian era home of a wise, loyal group of friends whom I will forever respect and love. These poems are dedicated to the Katō Family of Katano, Osaka, Japan. You filled a boy with kindness, philosophy, honor, and multitudinous books when he was trying to become a man. Here is to Dinners of Wagyu beef and plum wine in heaven somewhere along the remains of Hirokawa Temple next to Saigyō and Sei Shōnagon on our next cycle through life together.

Love,

M.C.

2019

TABLE OF CONTENTS

加藤

When I go,
Guard my tomb well,
Grasshopper.

-Issa Kobayashi

For the Dogs Knowing I'd be Raised by Women

Nebulae bloom and stars arise.
Helium flashes. The sun dies.
Eyes pointed up, I saw dawdling
Glints of resurrected fire.
Leftovers of giants burning at
10,000 degrees Kelvin flickered
In the black November sky,
Proving I might still be alive.

I was twenty, feeling fifty.
My black lab cried for her meal
And the moon crept south for winter.

Last week I found my calling.
So I wrote my dead father a letter.
As I scribbled, moonlight jigged
On a far off Catholic gravestone.

Maybe the stars are time itself
And time too is endlessly born.
The dog just eats her kibble,
Thinking not of stars, space or
Of the infinite meld of it all.

For dogs, time is nothing.

One Day in Katano

Mama,
I write you from a hell
I hollowed out
25 years denying. Though
Now I know it is very real.
I bowed here to Jesus
Thinking of all the Japanese
Ways this afternoon - and used
Formal emperor speak with a
Polite policeman from Okinawa
And let me tell you. When I bowed
To him of the cuff and the gun
As the deer you love like stream
Waters flowing from Hirokawa to
Hirakata, he Bowed back to me fluently
Loving his and your mother, I thanked
My dear old dead dad then, because despite
His trip through the samsaraist milky way,
Becoming perhaps a Missoula blade
Of grass, he is blanked to time, but not
Here because everyone one in my heart
We Livin' livin' livin! as the stars are dead
Out in space, but to us we see bits of light
Dancing, naked, cold fire reds, indigo burners,
Seen radiating life, yet afloat in intergalactic
Cemeteries, buried in the void, the way we will
Be in eternity. Here in my hell, mama, we was
Raised by matrons abandoned and
Fighting the world alone. Like you are now,

Against men and the world, our moms fought on.
So our hell is home, you got that?
Later on down the lunch line, we left school,
After our snicker-doodles and pudding packs.
We checked into hades and it was sweet then.
Despite having nothing but bare bulbs
And four insular walls. Minus the stinky fart joints and
Ramones albums it's a bit like prison now
Where three magnetic locks, two steel gates,
Two oceans and two thousand years
Separate you from me and the red marker in my ear
You laughed at so much because it looks
Silly in your country. Whereas bards in my home
Are slaves to the muses, in Wa tanka scribes see
Grasshoppers at Jinja and pray on that moment,
Toasting rice wine to thirty-one syllables Saigyō
Would have laughed to heaven at, wadded
Into little trash baseballs and given to
Neighborhood children as gifts. But the pens,
Markers, pencils, brushes, blocks of carbon ink,
Stolen portrait mirrors, and teeth gnawed, yellow
Number twos, they are the Omiyage, tokens
Of my work as a silly ignorant bombastic ambassador
Poet in the heartland of Himiko San.
My god and carrying that much stationary
It cost me blood, hair, my safety and pride to
Get you this message, though
It's alright mama and don't you dare
Think twice about it because you,
As the ditty-dotty-ing larks, are never a burden
On my heart, you just fly, looking
For the sun each day, knowing

Fools lay in jail cells, waiting for little
Signs etched on the walls from you
In your past life. And exile aside
I'll wait until the soil stratigraphy
Molts again and only curly cued
Hollowed out fossils remain of us
Then I'll return to the heartland
Limping, ailing, scarred, illiterate now, having
Lost my mother tongue
Half dead. Yet gawking at moons,
Sleeves a-drip with booger-snot and
Tears, howling, I hope you'll be there
Under the waving flints and have
A way of lighting my descent home
Because we met among the hearty Taiko
Drum beats and cacophony of Sake
Aside the monks of Katano in a Fall
Men in white coats tell me never happened
To us at all. Yet little boys in blue Kimono
Laughing at the Matsuri songs serve as
A reminder that the past, though a dream,
Cycles us back to the corn fields of my boyhood
And the rice paddies when your blue sailor dress
Flailed with the pacific winds of typhoon
Season in one lifetime or another.
Sleeping I hear the final train pulling
Into a station outside Kawachi in gray rain,
I'm skimming Rumi and the red pen in my ear
Turns to blue just the way Miyazawa Kenji
Said it would and I know it now -
You love the wild lunatic Sunflowers
Just as I do mama
And more too.

Pangea the Archipelago

To you,
My rogue wave
Who rolls,
Crests nearly to the Pleiades
And breaks
On the archipelago
Beaches
Under the cheese colored
Waning gibbous moon
From the pacific
Nearer to me
From our dreamy
Eternity.

I, the beer stained
Tuxedo wearing
Drunkard

I am
Given the
Cormorants and lightning
Bugs, the big old
Royal skies
Of infinity.

I, the truculent
Boy of snivels
And pride
Plagued with
Ego still a
Fool

Am bequeathed
From the gods
The smells of
Wet black labs
And frightened
Squirrels chasing acorns
As their prairie hare
Cousin burrows her home
In the Beaumont soils
Of the slow rippling
Flints.

Among gifts of Ra
And Dionysus,
It is your love mama,
Your dinner biscuit shaped
Feet and peach
Skin, I envy
Most of all.

After a thousand
Fiery deaths,

Births in all
Earth's corners,

To all the land's
Benevolent mothers,

It was us I think,
That were ignited
Like the quasars, fused
Destined to erupt
Into the invisible
Conundrum of time.

Ponder it.

Once you happened,

I was forever.

My Silly Religion Love

I knew because somewhere a Lakota-Sioux
grandmother looked like you and your
Eyes flashed blue and then black and
You made my cowardly side descend away to
Places I'd never slip or fall to again in that
It mattered not where inside the silica
Ball of a world we live in, I'd dedicate enough
Of these silly songs to you that you'd poke
Your head out of the the hidden foliage
Eventually. If I wrote my own Bible dedicated to
You then eventually after a few millennia,
You'd have your own religion mama, and you my
Savior would be god not just to me
But to all mere children walking around lost
Unsure of what move to take next. Because
Of your good book, they'll have peace.
Understanding it all. And Wakan Tanka
Sits next to granny upstairs next to Andromeda
Scribing the lyrics to songs we've yet to write.
The seer, she knows hysterically chuckling
That the captivating lovers are ingrates and vagabonds
Wandering from Kansas to Kansai, in love with the
Heian cherry blossoms in spring and appalled by the
Weeping rains of autumn, drunk, alive, never dead
On repeat to the end.

Lost and Found at the Fall Matsuri

And we met collided at a festival
Which was surely named after you

You approach softly kind and
Accompanied buy a funny monoglot

Man you've been translating
For since before he could ever

Have seen you the way I do now—
Like all the waltzing stars of Orion's belt

Crashing right before my childish
Eyes. Like the defective New Year's

Fireworks of my childhood and the
Memories of heavy-handed step-

Dads—your kid-like rose colored smile
Wiping away the thick fog of the past

All of that—my heart in bandages but
Healing. As the ash black haired

Kids Sprint and play tag to God knows
Where and billow wild laughs

Smarter than us.

Defunct Magazines and Babies

Today I sent word to a publisher
of a magazine - Long out of business,
Informing them I'd like to subscribe to their

Defunct Wrags, but it
Turned out the thing left print just about
The time the Beatles broke up and
The flowery revolutions were over, and
After the addicts had to get their jobs back
On Terra and the earth kept rolling round
And created from nothing my generation
And we still call ourselves bards, proud.
Poor, addicted to all, skipping from pill
To pill.

But still, you have to appreciate an
Origin that's as old as the birds.
And their songs we listened to
Weaving sonnets and choka imitating
Sounds most men abandoned
In the forest, melodies left for
The clouds. Doomed. Remembered,
Whistled over skewers of Yaki-Tori
Chicken and dancing to the moon.

Songs Like the excerpt I skimmed now were
Doomed to warehouse crates and other
Frightening encapsulations for small exceptions
Like the one I had in my hand, the title
Not important or significant enough to
Remember. Something
By Shuntaro Tanikawa when he was a
Boy.
And the poems made me
Cry without crying.

Most likely never to be read - like me -
The books the publisher may have forgotten
To sell, probably would never see the eyes of
Small red children looking back into the words
And the woods,
Absorbing everything. It's what I thought then
The sun in my eyes.

I left the magazine on a Wichita park bench
knowing babies may cry and make
Daddy's Work shirts wet,
And that they are your survival and mine.
So their education and its pertinence for me is the
Unknown factor, who you marry, who and what,
You reach ecstasy among, matters
Little if the children can only say mama
In one language.

It's the words, the little curvatures,
The twister-cyclone blots
Of ink that eventually become
The babes we are so in awe of, with their
Ever-protesting brains. They. though unread,
Hold answers to the suns, stars, moons, dark energy.
The words like the babes, grasp it, why the
Grasshopper lives on a stone Buddha
At Hirokawa temple Its whole life dying happy,
Discerning the quadratic confusion of Tennyson's verse,
And everything
Else.

A Monk in Doubt in a Bar

A monk strolls into
An Izakaya bar in the Osaka
Train station, orange robed,
Covered in sweat, looking incredulous,
And gives us all a sermon:

The sound of prayers end
In an instant and we never
Know if our ceaseless chants
Aimed toward God have saved
Any one on Earth at all. Yet
We March to the temple-solid
With stream waters rinsing first
Our left hands then our right ones,
Splashing our age cracked cheeks.
Each morning waking resolute
Before the sun and the deer.
And we pray, appeasing, talking
With Yakushi Nyorai about Zika virus
And AIDS and about how poverty still exists-
He refuses To tell us monks why the
Gods watch people cry-waiting.
Never do his answers arrive but through
The bird songs. Oh the horrific
ambiguous beauty in the responses of our
God of well being and good fortune.

Still the day begins again and
The monks have an inkling—
Perhaps the sutras do mean something.
Though what, only blind babies
And tadpoles will ever know,
Keeping nirvana to themselves.

I think for now though,
I'd like to pay my tab, the nameless monk said.
The gods frown upon this sort of thing.

A Word on Mom

The ancient hebrew translating
Single mom of five begins her
Evening after dishes and beef burgundy.
Furiously transposing interdependent clauses
That bite at her notions of how we discern

Each other's words from gibberish,
The *Tawagoto*, which as it turns out according
To a Mukashi-Banashi singing Kenji is the
Real pedagogic gold Through which flies the
Intergalactic medium of Silicon-dust chunks
And cocoa pebble looking asteroids that'll

Sooner or later be careening down on scribes
The world over, stamping us out, but
Never the definition of the word mother
And how though we may keel over
Extinct from heart attacks and hoagies yet still
Everything will either be or have come from
A matriarch Sirius star giving all, to all.

Tawagoto is a Japanese literary term for nonsensical or parodied language.

Pretty Sakhalin Food

In experience it seems that being
Around a thing in general—like Dutch
Beer or Kowloon Cantonese grammar—
Pulls strong one's mind with a weird energy
In the general direction
Of adeptness at engaging with the magnetic soul of
The object-subject at hand. It's a bit gravity like
That way. The sun pulls pluto back
Into its core one millimeter per year
Or some such figure unknowable
By me, the hapless bard, and in
Lassoing the satellites—the people
Of many tastes, colorful touches and
Infinite facial geographies of anger-
Happy interaction that make up the
Other forms of gravity independent of
Mr. Newton—And the closer one abides,
Rising to meet doppelgangers far
And away and around the world again
And Again until Latin, Sanskrit, Cyrillic,
And Minoan Linear A meet up again and
Discuss how we fucked it all up so much when
It came to branching off with wars and gods
That we fissured the words we use to capture our
Food and that of the other when ours runs dry,
So irreparably that many of us will never know the word

For love or understanding when a feather
Hatted man cooking Unagi Eel in Sakhalin
Says *I do in fact understand love, thank*
You for trying so hard sir to shyupeak my
Langrrage," Bowing like Amaterasu once did
For some reason. Why? Because our subjects
Aren't as insular, alone, Discerning, and
Xenophobic as we, the real
Aliens, tried to cookie cut them out to
Be. They're just people speaking, cooking,
Staring at pretty, black haired lovers who
Hope to draw themselves in nearer and warmer, a hell of a lot
like pluto to the sun ball Buddha after a
Seafood dinner for a smell of life, of possible
Multiplication of that thing we call legacy,
That is really just cells and proteins multiplying.
We like names and call it romance.
Tisk-tit-titty-tisk. Will the gravity Ever
pull Em together, the people here at home?
I'd say it depends on the color of the evening
Cumuli, and the look on her face, which may or may not
Gravitate towards lips how some laws
say they should.

Catharsis Letter

Every day here, the first sun the world and
the Ainu carpenters ever saw, Rises. It is
the happy-sad 7-11 cashier not getting to see
it today,

To whom I write this letter.

Dear sir,

In the gilded Ray's this
morning, It is you who I respect
most.

P.S.

When you try and climb this mountain one day while writing
    poetry please, please be careful.
You might be late for the show or worse, miss the thing
    entirely forever.

Sent from my iPhone

Train Ride Reflection

As I ceased leering at my own face,
A sweaty reflection in zooming express train
Windows at dawn, I leaned in to see tiny
Jump ropers on the street outside the cross
Town locomotive that peers everywhere from
East burrow to Osaka Bay in endlessness, its
Fingernail dirt encrusted windows having seen
All matter of domestic wretches board the line-
And knowing, the image of myself in that window
Was nothing but a creation of my distorting eyes,
Projected onto the movie screen of my mind—
Where deadbeat dads and spouse beaters
Looked each night on the way home from Mills,
Breweries, Mines and DMV's, ignoring the
Kids back home alone, TVs as friends and
Onset acute loneliness waiting in the wings—
I snap eyes from Matt's face reflected, back
To the side-walk skippers, trolloping 5th avenue
And I see myself, little again, yet ancient, knowing
That in knowing reflections are not to be trusted,
That as the Sun rolls back behind the Atlantic,
Tonight, I will sip warm tea, happy and old,
But oh so young.

According to the Science Doctor

I used to
Believe math
And Pacific Island
Syllabaries were hard.
Then Dr. Michio Kaku
And I met for an Earl Grey
Tea in my dreams.
It was there and then
He taught me about
Real hardness. A thing's
Solidity,
He said, had nothing
To do with difficulty
Incurred while learning it.
Ideas, just as
Emerald and Onyx do
And CO_2 and H_2O too,
They all have matter and
What makes up
Everything is all
Technically hard at
Some point along the
Line during this meandering
Production process we
Call Existence.

So basically, it's all hard.
And yeah, everything is
Tough. Sure. But doable.
Unequivocally so,
Mr. Kaku said in my mind,
Grinning.

Still Learning

弘川寺

9.29.18 HIrokawa Temple

I know now that god
Was born to flying bird calls
High above trickling
Autumn creeks as the Pagans
Learned it. Though Mountains are Small,
men will never be so large.

Isms and Fools

For learning nothing save for show and
Tell and how to wipe their own buttocks
Soiling their huggies with bits of a cyclic
Shitty carbon and corn mixture for dad to
clean up after a 16 hour work day, I Respect.

Babies ought to be taught on arrival to Earth
How to spot the practicing fools in a realm
Of radioactive isms whose goal it is to enslave
The primeval mind, to keep the boy, the
Girl, the ism labels this child, this baby, this
Toddler turned adolescent turned fake glasses
Wearing, pasted-on beard sporting maniac

The villians do this, and that too wherein we are
Sentenced to the eternal fate of the pigeon-hole
Of over the counter socialization, where the word
Special is synonymous with stupidity in failures
To understand that the meek minded would rule.
And a white donning Samurai lady told me
The simpler things are just better. Period.

And the babies they got it right again, leaving me
A trail to their future mama's front door only to
Have me walk in and realize that the finishings
Had been stolen and that if I wanted a bed, a crib,
Bookshelves, a dog-house, a bicycle

I had to do it all myself. And that sir,
Is teaching. The simple things can be given
And the solutions to the morning pears?
Well those answers may never be found
Not as long as we fight over things
Inconsequential to rivers.

Ezekiel: A Re-Write

14. I owe to you
My small wraths
In a place Ham looked
Upon his father's lewd
Body, not with shame
Nor pure lust or
With genital malice
I will sing of this
Science of sexual
Examination with
Various faces and in
Frenetic crowds round
The Earth and back
For him, for her,
For them, for you and
Especially you mama

15. And the cable news
Sirened for emergent
Bombs cast from the
Fertile crescent plain and
Weird alliances which fill
The pacific ocean with their
Ever dropping blue radiant
Tears -

And my god, she says, *A halt to*
All alarms, now kneel
For mama.

16. *If you should refuse*
The freedom of your childlike
Ears and give ignorance to
My warnings now, they,
The playful amongst you will
Cry out too. As if their precious
Fate lay forever doomed to
Hades' chasm for good.
So shall you weep
Our mother cried.

17. *I and my Satori*
Eye opening sex, the
Sex which fucked your
Fathers blind and made
Blood of kings east
And west curdle in infantile
Fear. I made you, she shouted.
Sisters and sons, daughters, and
Brothers. This is my work.
My art and you, my
Little dolls are that with which
I play and feel at ease.
I may lay vengeance at your
Feet from time to time,
But do not fear me now, Son.
Never.

Tempo of an American Heart

Please remember us, mom said, eyes white and wide
    as the moon.
Because like a big red slice of Wagyu beef, we, your
Compatriots now, will always be there. We vow as family.
Speaking not your mother tongue but thinking in it,
Telling jokes in our language and sympathizing
    with the beat
Of your heart which is so like ours, son.

Kenji Miyazawa Laughing

Be an iconoclast telling jokes
Instead of the mad man ever in rage
Who practices Kendo at high noon with
Madness and sweat pouring from your
Overworked, fragile bones.
Just ask the Salary
Man.

Mishima Yukio wrote philosophical
Edicts stark raving pissed off at
All the centuries precursing the new
Archipelago. He cut out his guts with
A sword trying to take us back to the
Good old days, knowing the beauty of
Blood and the nobility of the Samurai
Forever.

But,

Kenji before him scribbled wacky
Eyed children's books and entered class
Rooms through the sliding windows in view
Of the pink gardens. He died of tuberculosis,
Foregoing self-inflicted wars. He embraced
The natural ways of releasing the soul,
Without shifting the world in a direction carved in
Flames.

Robot Boy Reading

A sweaty shaking boy scans the pages
  Of a worn out copy of the Age of Reason.
He flips to yesterday's dog eared chapter
  On the mind being one's Sistine chapel.
How the Huguenots, the Greeks, and silly
  Zoroastrians, the Sephardics and Sikhs
Might have gotten it all wrong, searching and
  Scratching notes in margins, all capitals
Saying, *Could they all be wrong?..., Could*
God not have seen my Tumblr feed last night?

A Science Rumi Dreamt Of

If I were an astronomer
Of the night I would measure
The time between your navel and Europa.
I'd extrapolate the data behind
Fractured hearts and examine traces of you from
Mars-quakes on Olympus Mons
And I'd know why the moon dotes
At me with your globular eyes.
To a tee I'd find why time is mere theory
Here where my sinful lips meet your neck
And I don't know if Andy Goldsworthy
Could paint the soft science of you
In his momentary ices or rocks or
Malleable clays.
I simply know that I am and
That we are here.
That friends or lovers or foes,
Though we poets love, we are
Damned to event horizons
Of black holes so near.
Pulling stretching, tugging, writhing
Us into little forever longing
Spaghettified strings of
Never more tumescent remnants of stars.
These are concepts Rumi
Might have dreamt of but never understood.

Like we, the bards of time strived and failed
To know in solemn curiosity, to Distinguish
Whether or not Earth and lunacy
Adored tumbling round or not.
In all time asking how we might keep
Dancing in the Pleiades light
Till the skies have fallen and our
Sun grows dim.

Rapping Marco Polo With the Kids

I don't want to go on record
Here as saying that you can learn
Anything from anything, but
Once in a teeny El Dorado library,
I learned the term Didactic Language
Instruction Methodology from a pink
Children's dictionary with a deer
On the glossy floral patterned dusk jacket.
Difficult as it seems to be, the kids and
Their kiddish things might be teaching
Us more than sweaty old crotchety
Professors in pit stained sport coats,
Rapping Marco Polo
And Columbus. Our kids mama,
They will see right
Through it.

Her Own Master

I wake from dreams
Which are far less war related
Than yours were ma'am.

To you, crops was crops,
And it was all sugary
Corn stuff in the end anyway in Heaven.

And you had one master
But what I heard you saying
Cracked my heart and went like this:

I always had just one Massa and
Believe me sonny, that song singin' woman
In those fields was me.

And now

There were never any masters
In the world except for the likes of me.
You know that. Don't you kiddo?

A Polyglot Oriole

Hajimemashite, doko kara kita,
I ask the Oriole
Pecking dew ridden
Grasses on my front lawn.
I like to pretend the
Birds at dawn understand
Something not English.

Wondering where
And when the winged one
Had flown in
From this morning
As she flapped, soared
And cackled at Cessnas
On her descent into my
Dandelions with the sun.
I asked. She chirped
Silent.

Soon as I inquire
Her yellow mates swoop down
From the birch like spitfires.
Chirping and whistling mad songs
As if I had been rude.
I too would envy
Such a flyer
In the garden.

English Departments in Heaven

English departments in Heaven
Must be rather empty places,
Cold from cigarettes not being
Smoked. God never did like fire
Wielded in hands other than his.
And that's what I think as I brush
My teeth frantically, gums bleeding.
Considering that if I stay clean long enough
I'll find the beat of the wind and
Get into the pearly gates despite the
Yellow nicotine stains on my fingers.
Maybe clean teeth would keep me
From homelessness too. It was
Destiny to be poor singing these songs.
Perhaps god will rent me a room
One day where Constantine used to live.
Up or down there I'll stay.
Maybe I'll write love tankas to
My wife and she'll realize it
Back on on Earth where she'll undoubtedly
Still be when I'm gone.
No one is bad or righteous,
Destitute or destined for greatness.
No one is pure or wretched.
Most are just bastard men,
And that I really did love her
Too.

My Label, My Title
頑張れ

For Kaori Katō

Pertinacity is my name.
This is my power, mama.
I do not quit searching.
Ever.

Imitating Lorca

Focus, my dove. On the pothos.
Its leaves are whispering
A crying whisper
Sounding Polynesian death,
Sprouting,
Reaching for your hands
As I do for your heart. And
The Plant bows
To you,
Praying for summer rain.

Remembering Malcontents

Just know that flailing
People tend to get
Pissed off at the poorest
Amongst us who raise their
Hands often and ask too many
Questions that others mark
As irrelevant. Though it's
Not their fault. They only know
Apathy. But as we,
I have been just that desperate
For a meal of oats or for
Something bitter and mischievous
Like knowledge of Umami cuisine.
For some, the answers to classroom
Inquiry is like air and proteins.
We need to know in order to stay
Among the voracious and merciless
Food chain of gator skin shoe
Wearing maniacs on Broadway.
At stake
My loquaciousness goes on like this
Despite the malcontents:

Yes, excuse me? Ms. Teacher?

Question. Answer? Please?

Ignoring all others.

An Expectation

Under compositions of constellations
Whose light I was told had died out here
I suppose to my own ailing frontal lobe that all
Those thick books had answers that
You said would break me at sunset mama.
The Alamo's ashes must have been more
Than just knives and trickery from old
Texas and I remember their accent like
Father's. Irish and somehow Saxon I
Remember. Our daddy's daddy's gutted
Out fellow Anglo eyes with
Pocket knives that looked like mine. And
These urges now, not all that rare underneath
Rain, I am one of them and so too I fear
White smoke because though my mother hurls
Herself to the sky come dawn, I quiver and save
Bamboo twigs for shivs, wailing in
Tears and fear for the next warring period.
Knowing that I am headed for prison
Or bars in Osaka.

Commonality

Now I realize it. limericks, verse,
Lyrics, sonnets, Tawagoto, haiku:
All of them are pastimes of people
Who appear adult on the outside but
Remain children in their rapid hearts.
So when you meet one of us, take care.
We are quite gentle, yet razor-death
Sharp like the spines of a blowfish
In hunting starfish and minnow
Like in the vicious current of Hiikawa.
So as I weep at the sight of
Crickets, a garden sitting master Waka poet
Associate of mine might gouge your fucking
Throat out for taking issue with meekness
And
That's the thing. All the idiot poet
Bards always have tended to be friends
In the discerning unrhyming
World as the green insects tend to know it:
Beauty comes from the hearts
Of poor bastard monks
Begging on the
Cracked streets.

Something in Eternity

Everything ever written
Is a little eulogy
To someone or something
Which exists now afar
Or once existed like the
Pterodactyls and Geocentrism.
Your eulogy too, as your life,
No longer scares me because
You're alive somewhere
As a hot spring or
A gold eagle.
Content forever, sir.

September Blue

I don't know what you always cried
For Saigyō, but it must have been
Similar to tonight for me as for you
We are lost with only the blue Moon
Lit mountain peaks to guide us home
Again. And that home my friend, where
Is it now? Where, for in the west I am
A Middle age peasant and in the East I
Am but the debased man forced to
Constantly joke about to remain safe
And alive at heart. Where must I go in
Your Kansai plains, dear poet? In these
Horizons of peaks and fresh burnt rice
I dawdle, knowing how lost you must
Have been, friend. And the daily parades
Keep me happy and everyone reads here.
Both the tome and ticket of trade from
The Konbini. But we barely speak. Where
Is my home now? Anywhere amongst the
Autumn sun? For you were ascetic and
Suzuki San was the Bodhisattva in the west.
Then what am I but lost, bawling and blue?

Son of Andromeda

Like rifles' muzzles
My friend, your voice
Has thundered through
The gates of heaven.

I assume, riding the sea
Now and speaking with Shiva
In the psychotic flickers
Of snakes in Gobi desert flames

You strum your guitar to
The moon as it swims
Across the August sky,
Agreeing, you aren't dead
        Yet.

And I see the wren
Staring at a black lab you knew
Who gawks at the nibbling
Squirrel. All of them cloaked
        In sunlight.

It reminds me of the morning
Luck.

How my lungs steal
Breaths, airs bequeathed
As you once did, little
Parts of life borrowed from
Andromeda.

Interlude for Dad

Parked in front of the bar before work
I hear *Dirty Work* by Steely Dan on the radio.
Easing up the volume and breathing in lyrics
Not heard since through your ancient VOX
Speakers. I see the long, skinny, black cigars
You used to hide away and smoke
As I raced hot wheels on the shag carpet floor.
You'd pay me a fiver every time I caught you
Lighting up. A scent of black coffee and warm
Blunt tobacco embers spiraled in my nose then.
Damn, buddy. Caught me again you'd say as
I held out a hand. You always did pay up.
Your songs, no more though, our songs the diamonds
On black grooves, chirp-scratches on your
Treasured vinyl copy of *Highway to Hell* you bloodied
My nose for stealing. Clunking gears of a
Tone-arm rising, cutting the tune forever now.
And picks of 70's pop rock by Phil on KFXJ:
Pry, yank, force bits of joy and rage from my eyes.
It's your songs, our songs, your strange Abba phase.
Your obsession with Todd Rundgren albums,
Moody Blues cassettes and your withered
Neil Young *Decade* pressing and *Mr. Soul* and
Cinnamon Girl that kept me *rocking like a hurricane*
As Jesus on the cross, arms outstretched knowing
That you and mom were there as I met with Buddha
On Mount Hirokawa in Kanan and the grasshopper

Knew I was becoming a man, or maybe you all
Were hallucinations keeping the songs playing
In my head. You, burnt out Daddy-O, went to sleep
Forever before I left for the mountains, but
Your music and spirit never
Faded away.

War and Zazen

Cedar bristles sway.
In breathes the wild hornet.
Waves break with spring wind.

So the blue marble tells me.
God carved the horizons and
Hot protruding roads of man
Bring unrest, Zazen, and
Theological civil war
Here.

Mothers cry, sons part
Revolving seasons endless
Inform us too. God's voice
Led us here but never
Will carry us home.

That part is our job
To carry out in poverty.
Alone.

Celebration

After you left, mama,
Pop bought a .357 magnum
That he cleaned on the
Weekends while he sat
At the dining room table
And pined for you. That was
Until after years of sipping
Secret drinks, his kidneys
Failed while listening
To Elton John's *Rocket Man*
One night in Autumn.

He was sad like that. You
Could see how he'd been trapped
In insularity, his eyes glazed
Over from the thought of
You.

And he took his Cessna
Check every week, calling
It a golden life of labor.
Bought himself a fifth of
Corn moonshine every year
On his birthday. When was it?
What day? Time has stolen

Memories of those particular little
Squares on the calendar from
Me. I just know he wept
For you as if you'd flown
For the green of Borneo while he rotted
In the gutters of Hell's Kitchen.

I don't blame you though.
Any cliche bastard who would die
To an English pop singer on
The turntable was too blue
To spend eternity vouching for.

Similar Moons

Summer will hide your
Brown eyes from me
This year as I, a fool
Eyeing the grass grow
Will miss the Gerberas
Of a hilltop wind farm.
There you confided your
Heart belonged to seasons
Like mine. It was many
Colors ago, too many to
Clearly recall, as I trip
On life, blinded by ego.
I reside and wait here, a
Silly child on an oak stump.
Poor in respect to hearts.
Rich in trivial nouns and
Watching the moon. Knowing
You too will see it tomorrow.

Trotting

You, my friend begged. Free.
Gliding with the unknown
Winds.

East in winter high.
West in love with
A wanting

Greater than the rest
Of Fools

Trotting Earth poor
With wounds red and
Rich.

Envoy:

Now a Doberman
Pincher in Helena or
Little Rock, you howl
At her still, dead now.

Very much
Alive.

An Instructive Punch

The impossible is
Usually slow to
Be understood and

When asked about
Usually ends with
A fist to the cheek

As the Rinzai masters
Know it. Great feats
Come with suffering.

Impossibilities are quiet
too like The mighty
Arkansas Rivulets.

At least my medium,
That's what she
Tells me

Noting that if I just wait
For our galaxy to
Collide with the

Waves of Andromeda
Then on this Earth
The definition of impossible

Of deaths of dreams and
Births of wailing bards
Is for love and babies

Like us.

Mama and Papa

Wondering why in blood
Red Bic ballpoint pen, teachers
Assuage Our little kiddy mistakes,
I conjure all the reasons.
How do all these mamas
Keep proving right all of
Sigmund Freud's jokes?
They concern horny teenagers who
Want to lay with cougars at
The bright of noon who look as
Their mothers do? That tidbit of firm
Instruction is all the signpost
In the world I need these days.
Because Austrian psychologists
Don't know the same things all
The mamas and the papas out
There do. It was them
who made this poem
Possible. According to me, they
Are most certainly god.

De Rerum Natura with a Handgun

Lucretius said nothing
In *The Nature of Things*
About the bullets that would
Make my friends disappear
Like the oceans that used
To roll over the flat
Dormant flint hills now.

The Orwellian history of now.
The comets, corrosion,
The cultural eutrophication
And police officers murdering
Sick men, the elderly mad
And the poor. They've rotted
This land through the years
While automatic weapons
Filled the supermarkets
And the children lost their tiny minds
To the whirling rusty storms
That are manufactured
In our soot filled skies
Which are only indigo
By illusion.

Though, I find myself unafraid
Of spring twisters, flash floods,
Droughts, grain famine and the
Genocide of bees in comparison to
The legalities of carbine rifles and
.50 caliber ammunition rounds
Constructed for the purposes
Of invasions and mass fratricide.
For what are we but a genus
Of siblings warring over the
Definition of god?

That the rot minded child
In stunted growth may barter
For glocks with hair triggers.
That a manic depressive may trade
A few crinkled twenties
For an army surplus hand grenade
Carried by a now dead soldier
Who served on Khafi '91.
That the monsignor might spend
The collection plate donations
On a pump action shotgun,
Wiping out the choir boys at
Sunday church in the Magdalene for
Being one Hail Mary short.

These things are why Heraclitus
Might have gotten it right.
Perhaps all the basic elements of life,
Earth, the cosmos and the psyche have
Derived themselves
From fire.

A Word from Friends

We only see Christ through pulsing stars.
Gawking at the cross to the south,
Civilizations died, blinking out small lives.
Little microbe men on Jupiter's moons know not

That the polar sow went hungry
Last night as the Toxodera napped,
Perched on the wilting reeds
On the wrathful Mekong river.

Whether god is dying or dead
The restless, angry current swells on us all.
In its raging, swirling, crashing voice it says,
My friends, Earth she whirls maligned.

And the dicots, the cottonwoods blue
Nevermore are green. Their cousin,
The willow whispers to me at sun up,
Jesus was a man just like you.

—

The lark never prays for rain like you.
She just knows that it's coming.

A Special Diet

On an old paperback of *Leaves of Grass*
There amid the pages ripping the spine
Are the gnaw marks of my pet cottontail.
Artemis, we named her. She dines on books.
And I think how poignant quadrupeds are.
Timmy hay, twig of pine or book of poems
Carelessly tossed about her realm, the floor.
It's quite all for her hungry small heart.
Then I think how funny and natural,
A rabbit eating Walt Whitman like that.

They Grow Up

Today,

My wife sold
Her mother a
Bottle of methadone
For thirty-six
Dollars and her
Promise of love.

At a diner
Sunday morning

I watch and feel sad
As the pregnant mother
And her four kids sing
To a glowing pink cake.
While I sip coffee,
It's a small girl's
Birthday.

Thinking of my wife and
And the brown pigtails
She once had.

I wish in silence
Something like prayer.
That these babies, as she,
Won't have to pay
For hugs and kisses
With cash and drugs.

And tears.

One day.

Babyl Relic

Three neighbor children
Barged like wind into my house
One day while Chuck Berry
Was playing Memphis, Tennessee
Through the Spirit of St. Louis
Speakers.

They were triplets, all girls
And a peculiar thing happened.
Each sister began to dance.
The youngest smallest looking
One curiously inspected the turntable.

All their little arms were writhing
With the rhythm and their miniature
Bodies moved to the king's
Twelve bar groove.

It was cathartic
To see children who were born
During the Obama administration
Look at a record machine as though
It were a relic of Babylon.

Experiencing the whole thing
Led me to question whether or not

There is a time table on
Youth and innocence.
When do we stop dancing to
The music? When does nodding
Your head and tapping your
Foot not cut it anymore?

At a certain point somewhere
Between the eighteenth and
Seventieth revolutions, we seem to
Lose sync with the inner pulsar
That has made our souls work since
Birth.

And I'd like to blame the landlord
Or the minimum wage employer
For sucking away that youthful
Openness to feeling a song as though
It were a fine linen and kicking
Back with amenable young ears.

Amid the guitar chords and jigging
Though, I can only thank the stars and
The parent nebulae. For the jovial twirling
Triplets, they haven't grown out of
Happiness yet. They're young still
And liberated as the falling leaves,
Nothing more. Picket fence
Smiles too.

Friend Far From Home

The Aussie monk
Said to me smoking
A joint on a Hirakata
Park bench in a breeze.
It was the opposite end
Of the world and the
Smoke was different
Here. Like rice and wild
Sunflowers. And he said:
Marijuana is less of
A drug and more an inhaled
Food which helps open
Satori a bit quicker, mate.

*Satori is a term in Buddhism which refers to the opening of a third
eye. In this apparently rapturous moment a human being is said to
attain all encompassing enlightenment and wisdom regarding the
perceivable world. There are multiple means by which one may
experience this onset of enlightenment. However, for the context of
this poem, it is best to think of Satori in the way followers of the
Sudden School of Zen Buddhism know it. In one moment a human
is lost and ignorant, separate from the physical world, and in the next
he or she has no conception of being lost and is but a part of the
precipitate organism of the world.

Thesis on Rain

The crack in the vinyl siding
Of my empty house
Collects sweat from the sky
As Big Blue sails around Earth
And the gaseous puffy trash bags
Rustle up in Heaven, damning
Up the long, long rays of yellow
Sun.

The willows are rambling now
Telling me that god has had enough
Of my bullshit and that of all his children
I was the orneriest one, that every time
He thundered from on high, the lightning
Was aimed straight for my mischievous
Heart.

The last confession I made was to
My dog though she hadn't asked for it.
I tell her I've cheated and stole,
Coveted and swindled and she gawks
At me panting thirsty tunes of
Whimsy with her upside down idiot labrador
Smile.

And the raindrops tick on maple leaves
At my front door. I see and hear and
Know their veiny parts are upturned
Like tiny wine glasses collecting the clouds'
Tears. Then I think how wonderful I'd be
At bathing and dancing in dollops of
Rain.

So it seems god isn't dead or alive.
He's just the idea of my brothers' imaginations.
That if we ever needed him, he would be
The precipitate. Our holy spirit would be the bits
Of aqua and rose that fall, birthing the
Maypops.

Father Son Blues

父子のブルース

For Jyugo Katō

In the vibrating sunburst
Horizon over rich aged
Mahogany, two trios of string
Sing arias and resonate blue
Like Kenji's tanka, except in
Pentatonic form. Your nickels
Take the beat of *Sweet Home
Chicago* and my wound steel
The recitative of Robert Johnson's
Leftover devilish heart flown to the
Kansai Plain, just for us.
Weeping angels envy this piece
Of timber and metal singers
Of poems, whose intonation we
Try over and over again to
Feel. And wide hands caress,
Loving them, stealing
Them, rapturing ears.
Oh, fair lute won't you give
Us the voice of the dawdling
River outside tonight?

More Rain

Mama, it's raining here now
And among the typhoons as you
Are these days, I know you would
Enjoy it. I'm alone here listening
From the window and the pink
Curtains flutter. Opposites sure
Are are funny like loving the sun as
God and knowing you smile at the
Pitter pattering raindrops on the
Eaves. We work to find the reason
For tears as the child learns the sky
Can cry for him and he writes letters
Home to find the bread crumbs again.
And some god from where you are
Told me tonight. Hearts are strong like the
Quaking Earth and we know it too.
These little notes are in the beads of
Rain, falling here in spring as they do
In the archipelago dancing atop your
Umbrella.

Logic of Wind

If the pines sing in breezes
Then their roots aren't yet scorched.

If the falcon wings back north in March
Then Greenland must not have melted yet.

If the sun roves back to its zenith
Then today, humanity might survive.

If today is called Tuesday by us humans
Then the grass must still be growing.

These are mantras to logicians
Who speak in Xs and Ys and ifs and thens,

Who miss the beats of the wind and
Who misinterpret the sun

And simplify the prairie birds
And Shepherd willing pupils' eyes

To their own pointing fingers,
Diverting them from the moon outside tonight.

Greed in Tanzania

My Tanzanian friend
Informed me that cops
Back in his home
Country are quite
Easily corrupted.

One morning he was
Caught speeding and
Found himself able to
Buy off one of the pigs
With 200 shillings and
A slice of buttered bread.

It seems these
Officers are a lazy
Kind of crooked. They
Will demand a pay off
Of Grandiose proportions.

Then they'll settle
For whatever you have
In your pocket and send
You on your way.
It's sweet really, greed
And sympathy all wrapped
Up together like that.

¼ Sioux Aspiration of a Lifetime

Ultimately my goal
Was to half ass being
A news journalist with
A bad paycheck
Who spent fifteen minutes
Writing articles and
Seven hours researching
Archaic synonyms for
The word mother—
I never could capture
Just the right one but
Regrets are best left to
The wind my *Unci* always
Says at the nightly dinner
Of Cup-Noodles while in the
Past Her *Unci* in bliss white
South Dakota under the freezing
Hot sun, chomped rabbit ass—
These words of my family
Ignore the facts of newsmen in
Pinstriped insolent suits.
My family was allocated to
Oklahoma firework stands and
Tobacco shops selling back
Cancer to the white man.

And these words aren't so
Archaic I think. Once my *Unci*,
My mom's mom, was called
That. It was her title like a
Star. In charge of the little
Ones, a queen, a source for
All life. Her loving and diligent
Tears were on Earth
Quite for good amongst
The prairie dirt.

Caucasian and Homeless in Beijing

These are the sounds I dream

The squall of a single erhu bowed
Sings ancient low notes and
Trickles eastern voices from
The peak of mount Lingshan

With the cries of Sakamoto's piano
And the pleasant murmur of my
Dog's snore as she dreams of
Ham bones and unborn puppies.

These are the sounds I dream
When I think of waking homeless
One morning in the streets of Beijing
With no knowledge of Mandarin.

It wouldn't be so foreign.
English too, being soaked and
Tainted with pernicious slandor.
Some sounds though have no language.
My fellow beggar laughs making it true.

American nor Chinese tongues
Speak with the volume, the weight
Of stringed instruments
Or sleeping dogs.

These are the sounds I dream.

Railroad Teaching Me Life Lessons

Life whispered to me as I
Walked the train tracks east,
Giving me breaths and secrets
My cell phone never does.

The slight pink of dusk wind
Quilted over my face and
As the monarch butterfly landed
On a stone, becoming stone,

I questioned the insular life
Of humans. How singular we are.
Lonely, small
People we are
With weapons, oils, and god.
Among my backyard
Tenants of deer and oak.

Along the train car path
Sauntering. The sun yawning for bed
In the west on the other end of the
Earth

I learned from life never to throw
Rocks into the crowded woods.

It might scare the doe
Nibbling at honeysuckle.
A cast stone can orphan the fawns.

Funny, my voice has an echo
In the forest, along these
Railroad tracks at sunset.

Late Bar Biryani

Once over Biryani
In Mumbai's Big Bang
Bar around what I
Thought was clasing
Time. Quarter to
Eleven or so I think.
I waved down and begged
The undernourished
Looking server's pardon.
*When is y'all's shutting
Time,* I asked. The waiter
Locked me into his line of
Sight and said, "Sir we don't
Close until 25:00 o'clock.
And then, realizing that
Apparently in India, days
Last longer than twenty-four
Hours for some reason and
I had a king's share of naan
Bread slathered with tahini
Paste and garlic to crunch down
Into my stomach. I replied with
A, *Dhanyavaad** and knew then
There are definitely worse
And far more frightening

Prospects in life than hand eaten
Indian cuisine and the smell of
Fire roasted bread from
My lovely friend's kitchen.

Thank you in Hindi

Her Cartwheels

Mother she burnt
Shades of jet
Black that night.

Lightning
Zigzagged and
Struck the house,

Bruising that
Olive skin
Of hers.

The scars eroded
Her face into a
Dry Riverbed.

She was an
Invisible
Specter and I say.

Your blood
Was infused
Again

With ether
And
Gasoline.

You heard the echo
Of Tumbling because
It was you.

A girl cartwheeled,
Slung down the
Stairs at midnight.

Forever turbid.
Frigid.
Dead. Lost.

Windows shatter,
Burst to
Silvery scraps.

In sleep
You sense tickling
Dribbles of blood

Swimming eddies
Through
Your gaunt fists.

Tanka on Heaven

As scribes it's
What we do, scream
Weap, guzzle sake
Then stare at moons
Even though there's
Only one around
Here anymore.

Pondering a time
Pre-late heavy
Bombardment as
The astrophysicists
Call it, when lunar
Cratered pearl satellites
Danced in the solar
Ballroom in drunken
Wild orbits bounding.

Could we have been
The ash on Earth
Waiting for Tanka
Verses from ferocious
Suzano in the sea
Discoursing on Heaven?

2018 Halloween Party Costume

For this year's harvest festival in Osaka
I couldn't find anything gorey enough

Or that scared me to death quite well
In order to call it a good and festive

Costume. So I just found old dusty
Clothes and everything all the dead people

I know used to wear and use daily back
Then. There was for example straight

Boot-cut black jeans and the red plaid
Button ups my father used to wear to work.

Then there were the navy blue Converse my
First poetry teacher gave me in junior college.

He'd wear them in class with a sport coat
To piss off his boss who preferred the

Faculty to wear loafers or non-slip Doc
Martins. He was a genuine punk and as

A lost boy in Japan, it was rubbing off
Onto me I think. Whatever that means

And more. In a historic sense, I was god
Damned scary, the spirits rising in my heart.

They were Bodhisattva warriors back when
I thought no one good died and became the blue
Sky.

On Family, Mountains and Cycles

A kindness worn by you
And your family saved my
Life once and then again over
Raw eggs and warm rice this morning.
I ate, hungry, loyalty coming now.

And it's winning my undying love
Every day as I see the eyes
Of the stray cats you groom.

As the world knows I was once homeless
Too, like the angry tabby-cat
You nursed back to opulent life.

I grow strong with knowing
That you reside among the mountains
You sang of and taught me

So well. Father, mother,
Brothers never gone, I glow here in
America away, knowing your
Presence still as the ghosts.

In my heart you are never lost
But ignited from here until we

Meet amongst the deer of
Tōdaiji when Earth's magnetic poles
Flip again and we are brought
To each other in love and
Familial tidings
Once more in
Samsara.

Polytheistic Advice

I'm Catholic
I'm Buddhist
Too
The Vietnamese
Girl Said
From the seventh floor
Of a psychiatric hospital
In the wee hours as
My Cymbalta kicked
In.
The cross
And Zazen
Will save you
She said with
Her black
Onyx eyes.

The Candelabrum

This morning I woke
And the first thing
That hit my eyes
Was the candelabrum
On top of the armoire
In our sunny master bedroom.

All four flames still
Glowing from the night
Before reminded of the
Love we still managed
To oscillate amongst
Our fissured quaking hearts.

As the dreamstate faded
A candle attached to
One broken arm of the
Fixture — It had long
Since been destroyed,
Swept up and pieced back
Together with a weak
And cheap glue—

The flame blinked
Out and set loose in its wake
Toward the ceiling a spiral
Shaped plume of smoke
That smelled like maple.

It felt like us, like something
Was lost forever now. As if
Home had shifted to mean
That wherever you were
Is where life would go on.
And the smoke was a dying
Of the past we cried to the
Moon for. There we lay
Drifting back together.

Giving up Love and Bugs

To give up loving would
Be as for the ants roaming
The sidewalks outside,
Carrying birch leaves a
Hundred times their weight,
To abandon their plants
As food and burrow home.

Bugs live romantically simple
Lives and yet we love
And fuck and kill
And shoot up and knock down.
Dragging the homeless to gutters.

And we shop for soups and
Meats in cans as the
Eight legged people gather
Flecks of dirt and
Cedar bark to eat while we

Lie to our wives about the other girls
And play the stock market an illusion.
And watch reruns of Married with Children
And spend the rent on pot.
And name
And perform cunnilingus
While dreaming about this love thing.

All this happens while the ants
Secretly know the Indian proverbs
And skim Rabindranath Tagore underneath
Earth and think of man's frivolity
Bugs, with their joy and lightheartedness
And timidity, they know
The human condition of fear,
Like their own, has an air of petrification.
They know.
I think the arthropods and millipedes
Do too. They know it.
The monarchs and dragonflies.
Moths, Junebugs and fire ants;
They get it all. They must.
The little footed creatures
Of the world know.

The planet spins too
Fast to every really be understood.
They know with their antennae and
Pinchers.

To eat an elephant, a man, like a bug,
Must do so one bite at a time.

Jet Lag and Ieyasu

Sweating over rice in a communal kitchen after a twenty hour flight
It's funny to me, I thought. The residual imperialisms and stamping out
Of Unajuu and corn eating peoples where Ieyasu reigned and
Montezuma slept once awaiting without knowing it, fat old
Bombs to drop from western Heaven, For the Spaniards to march
On Lima and for their mamas' languages to disappear forever.
We humans have intuition when the stars are about to fall and
Little apocalypses are coming from the sea as they tend to do.
The I-Ching sakkas and Nostradamus types told us of it too.
And history's dead relatives call out to me over a cup of Nihoncha:
You must choose English no matter what your mother tongue is,
The DMV clerk shouted in my face on my sixteenth birthday.
Snap to an Osaka fall and, *Eets Jet yahg,* My Peruvian friend Carlos
Tells me in an English I know he wants to shout in Kechwa. *I cannot*
Syeep mehn, he trails and mumbles off in Spanish. He's tired of
Flights, cold weather and romance.

A Plus and Minus

Are lovers so different
Than magnetic poles?
Grasping each other's hilly
Curves from 10,000 miles
Away? We turn one thing
Into another into another
And back into love, The
Way space and time decay
Precious metals and minerals
Back into pure energy and
Forever. We, playwrights
And machinists make fate
Where haughty magnets are
Bound to Newton's rule book,
Their bible.

He Who Makes a Guitar

The luthier knows where he stands
As the Georgia dogwoods, he too
Shall pass away. The arbors like the
Master lute maker will spread roots
Through the crust of Terra one day
After creating life and music for all.
Each vibrating the soil as nickel
Reverberating above the rosewood
Fretting. Asked to define the word
Song the luthier whispers to his
Journeyman assistant. Whittle a viola
Bridge beneath a Makassar tree my
Friend. Then you will know. Songs
Are nothing but gravity, wood and
Metal scrambled together by us for
Dancing under the sky.

What If?

If the falcon could be wind again,
He would be.
If the chicken could turn back to limestone,
He surely would.
If the Kami tortoise could be the blue currents,
He would be.
If the bison could be maize and soil again,
He would be too I trust.
If the Man-of-War jellyfish could reside on

Seafloors once more as a rainbow fungi
Filling the stomachs of decomposer protozoa
Who would a millenia later be monarchs of the
Flint hills and ministers, emperors and oil men
After that,

He surely without a doubt, would too.

If my chocolate lab could hunt again,
Freeing herself from me to live in the pasture
And chase raccoons, she would too.

Maybe I'm the falcon, or once was and
Everything else on the planet too.

Odd Philosophy

For example today my Anasazi friend and I
Taught each other how to spot the criminal
Differences between tests and context.
In the next lesson—over dining room moonshine
In the rain at dusk, wind gusts pale horsing it past
The opened mahogany trimmed bay windows—
We explain-shout-debated the etymologies of
sympathy and Empathy,
We spent until the blue small hours watching the
Moon—realizing a truth which drives men to insanity
And Titan building civilizations to crumble—
It was about how you can have one without the other
But never Quite attain the other without the one.
And that's how we reached a sobering conclusion.
Because we'd dragged such flummoxing terms
Out of the dictionary Together, we probably had both
Of the latter nouns.

Aftermath of World Literature

Kurt Vonnegut taught me to read Ambrose Bierce.
Now I'm too sarcastic, calling newsmen lickspittles*.

Jim Harrison taught me to read Basho.
Now I'm too introspective and pithy, laughing at Hodgkin's
    Lymphoma.

Gary Snyder taught me to read Kenji Miyazawa.
Now I read Dr. Seuss looking for secret wisdom in his green
    pig rump.

Michael Cissell taught me to read Jack Spicer.
Now I know jackasses begin poems, but heroes and sea cows
    finish them.

Hemingway taught me to want to read Gertrude Stein.
Now as homeless friends call on sable moonless nights,
    I talk to myself, knowing nothing.

Stephen King taught me to read Krakauer.
Now I'm bathed in sweat, hunting the next story no one
    will read.

Bukowski taught me to read Pound.
Now I claim to be able to tell gods from titans, in Chinese.

Neruda taught me to read Vallejo.
Now I see the truth: all of us pick up the story, where the
    dead left off.

Mary Oliver taught me to read Lucretius.
Now I ask dogs the meaning of life and if Earth was molded
    in flames or monsoons.

J.K. Toole taught me to read Boethius.
Now I'm staring at whirling lollipop ferris wheels that
    remind me

Death is the price and the ticket to a ride
We've all ridden over and over and will rallph our guts out on
    until the yellow ball god flicks out

And the poets are left in the post microwave
Background radiation unemployment line

Where all the Gutenberg Bibles and copies of *Old Yeller*
Have been buried under ash from Yellowstone or a mad mad
    winter.

Devil's Dictionary page 77 of the 1958 Dover Press Edition.
It has a canary yellow cover and could once be found in the L.W. Nixon
Library At Butler Community College in El Dorado, Kansas 67042. Then,
my former boss, T***** M******** discarded it and the book now lives on
an oak, ebony lacquered bookshelf in my office slash hovel.

Black Furred Girl

I know when even the dog
Won't look at me that I've done something wrong.
That some moral crime has been committed.
That I've been rude to my wife
Or forgotten to say, *good girl,*
When she took my hand with her paw,
That I had drank too much wine
And stupidly forgotten to take her for a walk.
Of these kidlike foibles of the lout,
My black furred girl takes notice
More than anyone on Earth.
She smells it when I am acting
A fool.

And in these moments of foolishness
I'd trade it all for her kneading my hand
And to have known her as a pup.
As now, with her black face
And her beady maroon eyes,
Her small bark finding its way to the moon.
Just patting her head gives my life a purpose.
I adore her. Though as I sit alone
Outside tonight, the crickets
Chirp in verse and tell me that
Love only will never be
Enough.

After all, it was my wife who picked
Her from the litter.

Bother are in another room somewhere,
Angry with me and sick of being
In love.

Purpose of Learning New Words

Reading a book on Kansai, Osaka
Dialects I turn to my great *Unci,*
Her Sioux eyes knowing I've lost touch
With this world, chasing the next.
We understand each other that way,
Granny and I. She knows it took
Learning another family's slang and
Colloquials to figure out that in a way
We, Lakotah and the Ainu fisherman
Still trying to net Sama fish in Hokkaido
Creeks were always related children of
The sun. Whether or not worlds away
One of us was forking up spam and eggs
Before a day of farming, the other mawing
Fermented soy beans and Tamago for
Breakfast.

Both are family. Somehow the same
And our adjectives all were trying to
Teach babies the same thing. Hot meals
And hearts have a way of telling you
Something about families you never knew
You had out in the blue stormy world. That
A bowl of rice steamed by a friend thousands
Of miles from home was a kind of miracle.
This is what language was trying to tell
Us.

A Tip From You

For Kaori Katō

加藤かおりによると仕事と趣味と勉強は同じはずです。。これを聞いた時心の中大雨が降って平和が見つかった。。

Ms. you confided in me
This evening over shrimp
Spaghetti, sad, happy,
Thoughtful and stern.
Son, your work, your hobbies
And your studies should all
Be the same in this world.

And you smiled, forking
Noodles into your giddy
Smiling mouth, your lips
As always glossed in amber,
Confident yet cold. Your
Concern for it all. The helpless
Children under your roof and
The sun is and must be truly
Unmatched by everything but
The sunflower stalks in spring.
And my friend, a simple, *I love*
You mom, Takes the long form here
Again.

A Legacy

How I decided I
Wanted to be a teacher
Of first graders and
College freshmen
Goes like this.

A seven year old boy
In Katano with floppy long
Brown bangs draped
Across his baseball
Sized forehead in the
Fire light of the fall
Matsuri festival. The Kid
Looked up to

Me while I played guitar
Chords on a bench in
This Ancient park.
He said, having never
Met me and in English:

Sir, I hope you become
A teacher in my hometown
Some day. You communicate
So well. I wept that

Night over baked eel
On warm rice knowing
I'd been born in Kansas
But that my home was
In the land of Wa.

Answers in Poverty
円相

Because our revolutions will
Happen underneath quiet
Inauspicious looking trees.
In Hirakata parks, far from
My mother's shores, as things

Of great and grave importance
Are discussed over cheap beer.
That is how some and then all
Of the world will realize it.

Explanations of enlightenment
Are rarely, if ever, just given.

The winging egrets will never
Tell. You'll have to find the
Answers alone, mad, high
And with the love of friends.

Words at a Festival

I will write your festive
Coincidental name on
Calligraphy paper fifteen times
In three different languages,
From now until the sun
Draws close again, so
In that your voice and image
In my feeble brain is not
Forgotten. And that perhaps
One day, with karma helped
Along by that malcontent
Samsara, I might hear you
Tell me again in times
Of seeming tragedy.
Matto san, you are so
Good with kids. Let us
Meet again sooner
And not later. In Shibuya
Maybe. You are
Carrying so many things. Why
Don't you let me help. Don't
Worry anymore now.

A Sort of Influence

Today during a typhoon
Because I told a sad,
Pitiful story to her.

She laughed heartily.

And then

I laughed too.

Happy now.

Freedom of a Kind

A vagrant man can live
And cry hard at night.
Living long enough to
Ask why the titans in
The sky have taken
Everything away from
The helpless children
And more. To find a cue
The street waddler spends
His last two dollars on a
Notebook of scratch paper
For his little poems along
With a Payday for dinner.
He does this foregoing
Hunger, knowing scribbly
Didactic verse in times
Of poverty now, lead to
Freedom later, perhaps in
The next life when Earth's
Poles have flipped and the
Meek have inherited it all.
For now though, he's a bum
Waiting for the end of the
World. A man who will go
From a human being
To a three inch obituary in
A paper no one will read,
Having become free.

The Power We Have

I think I like What Teddy Roosevelt
Said. *Get action!* That was the
Glasses faced war hero's
Maxim.

That it wasn't about fucking is hard to
Understand, but I think it meant
Getting to peace standing atop the rockies
Looking west and finding truth.

It is said that the Bull Moose was a
Depressed man and that the disease
Interloped on his life so viciously he wrote
The Naval War of 1812 so it figures

Men driven to hopelessness wield a power
To drive out wild greatness if we only
Tap into it. A nose broken by dad can be turned
From pain into books and books of liberation
In the right kind of light.

The curious thing about depression is that
Sometimes it can be fended off using the
Windhorse mind. Forcing your brain to wander
A Thesaurus, looking for words synonymous
With agony and reshaping them into ideas
Of enlightenment.

As men with ailing heads there is no choice
In the matter, and wives suffer as the magnum opus
Is written in her honor. Every word an apology
Trying to redeem the irredeemable, the feeble poor.
Swallowing the world's tears we sing to your direction
In the world.

This power makes the hazy states of mind a choice.
Occasionally we decide what happens with the
Small spectacle of our lives, numb or not.
Happy or black and blue, jubilation laden
Or hopelessly condemned to howling at moons
Only the mad men can see.

With the ability to discern between living or
Perishing from sadness, therein lies picking
Between inhaling the scent of the purple Maypop
Or intentionally depriving the daisies sitting
On the kitchen window sill of water.

A Dog That Is

The dog drags her innocent tail,
Holding our love as she shakes, whimpering.
Then we see her trot across the moon,
Keeping our hearts taped and glued
Together from out there in space.

Her canine ears never blame us at all.
For wolves cant hold grudges.
Neither does she, with her cow bones
And peaceful snores in the afternoon.

In some ways she is our soul reverse
Anthropomorphized with four legs and furr
Clicking her paws on the marble kitchen floor.

She doesn't know how to feel sorrow or pity,
Anger, hate, irreverence, or greed. She just is.
So when spring comes, bringing us lust,
She just licked her butt, knowing it all.

Cycling Back

Basho's ditties about frogs could
Not have existed without you Saigyō and
The moon staring in through the hut
Windows each night back when all
We had to write about were glowing
Disks up in Heaven.

Like the Waka and Tawagoto jiberish
Scribbling masters before me, I sing on.
Knowing that in a way my parents
Were the real poets. That they created me
With a slight remainder hanging off
The chromosome that made me a silly
Asshole, barking at the east in broken
Japanese trying to find her heart
Again.

From Behind the Cell Door

This is the way I tell you I love how
Much shorter you are than me my sweet thing
And you are bigger. It's just that I'm small
Too. And you are smarter, my
Blood red and white mah-mah Matsuri.
In our language this means we clink shatter glass
Tumblers in joy. Though in my particular
Dialect these days, I am subject to
The prods of the judge because I happen
To love you still. One day, a spring morning,
I just loved you more than I can now. No,
I can't marry you as the sun comes up today.
But now here I am, facing captivity
Locked in a jail cell. And why?
Well, the reality is hidden from me too.
Perhaps mirrored to someone in harder
Love and in a more desperate land than ours.
Stone truth? Clarity is in the foolish lies.
The ring I etched our empathy into now gone.
In the diamond-less loop of sable jet black,
I told you I could be yours forever, but
We weren't ready, still watching the moon from
Inside the house. Not knowing, stars and rocks
Are mightier than us and it can't be seen until we circle
The Earth, knowing those with gravity
Like ours, come back to each other again in time.

Just now, we are star systems away, knowing the
Yellow flowers here and the pink bloomers there
All have seasons which align somewhere in time.
In time again I say it. I'll return to the spot in the hills
Where we held each other, stupid kids, heartbroken and
Blind. I'll go back like the basso-continuo of my silly heart,
Breathing in the same air you let into your lungs,
Knowing still, our monarchs fly together.

Envoy:

Life drips down in cycles, mama. It means I can Pilfer
The horizons for another century or so. Failing and
Tripping over it all. Knowing the rain that falls on you
Now will circle back round to me. A hint of you.

Because reality
Hardly seems real
Why assume
That dreams
Are really dreams?

- Saigyō Hōshi

Matt Cooper is a senior English major at Wichita State University and lives in El Dorado, Kansas. He has written for the WSU Sunflower Newspaper and has studied at Butler Community College and Kansai Gaidai University.

This project was made possible, in part, by generous support from the Osage Arts Community.

Osage Arts Community provides temporary time, space and support for the creation of new artistic works in a retreat format, serving creative people of all kinds — visual artists, composers, poets, fiction and nonfiction writers. Located on a 152-acre farm in an isolated rural mountainside setting in Central Missouri and bordered by ¾ of a mile of the Gasconade River, OAC provides residencies to those working alone, as well as welcoming collaborative teams, offering living space and workspace in a country environment to emerging and mid-career artists. For more information, visit us at www.osageac.org

Osage Arts Community